Love Yourself

21 Day Plan for Learning "Self-Love" To Cultivate Self-Worth, Self-Belief, Self-Confidence, Happiness

Stephen Fleming

Copyright © 2017 Stephen Fleming

All rights reserved.

Welcome On-Board: Get the FREE BONUS

I am privileged to have you onboard. You have shown faith in me and I would like to reciprocate it by offering the maximum value with an amazing gift.

As you are working towards improving your life consistently, I would like to contribute in your journey by offering a free bonus called "Health & Wealth Magnetism- Using the law of attraction to create Health & Wealth". It provides an interesting perspective to overall success and how health & wealth compliments each other to create a lasting success. I would be adding to this free bonus as I find other beneficial topics that can help contribute in our progress.

Type this link: http://eepurl.com/dglqCH
or scan below from your mobile

Copyright 2017 - All rights reserved.

This document is geared towards providing exact and reliable information in regards to the topic and issue covered. The publication is sold with the idea that the publisher is not required to render accounting, officially permitted, or otherwise, qualified services. If advice is necessary, legal or professional, a practiced individual in the profession should be ordered.

- From a Declaration of Principles which was accepted and approved equally by a Committee of the American Bar Association and a Committee of Publishers and Associations.

In no way is it legal to reproduce, duplicate, or transmit any part of this document in either electronic means or in printed format. Recording of this publication is strictly prohibited and any storage of this document is not allowed unless with written permission from the publisher. All rights reserved.

The information provided herein is stated to be truthful and consistent, in that any liability, in terms of inattention or otherwise, by any usage or abuse of any policies, processes, or directions contained within is the solitary and utter responsibility of the recipient reader. Under no circumstances will any legal responsibility or blame be held against the publisher for any reparation, damages, or monetary loss due to the information herein, either directly or indirectly.

Respective authors own all copyrights not held by the publisher.

The information herein is offered for informational purposes solely, and is universal as so. The presentation of the information is without contract or any type of guarantee assurance.

The trademarks that are used are without any consent, and the publication of the trademark is without permission or backing by the trademark owner. All trademarks and brands within this book are for clarifying purposes only and are the owned by the owners themselves, not affiliated with this document.

CONTENTS

1. Introduction — 1-2
2. Understanding Self Love — 3-8
3. 21 Day action plan for learning the art of Self Love — 9-43

1. INTRODUCTION

I want to thank you and congratulate you for downloading the book, "Love yourself - 21 Day Plan for Learning "Self-Love" To Cultivate Self-Worth, Self-Belief, Self-Confidence, Happiness".

Self-love greatly affects how we see ourselves. It affects how much we value ourselves. When you practice self-love, you see yourself as valuable and understand your worth; this helps you know you deserve respect and appreciation.

As unfortunate as it sounds, we live in a world where society has led us into believing that the best measure for self-worth is in terms of wealth, status, careers, sex, and power. In the real sense however, measuring yourself against these traits only raises more feelings of being inadequate. You end up immersing yourself in unending self-loathing. Learning to practice self-love will help you conquer this feeling and negativity.

To understand why you need self-love, you need to know what self-love is first. This guide will teach you everything you need to know about self-love. In this book, you will learn the difference between narcissism and self-love and how to love yourself unconditionally so that you can live a happier and fulfilling life.

Thanks again for downloading this book, I hope you enjoy it!

2. UNDERSTANDING SELF-LOVE

Self-love is an unconditional feeling of love and appreciation towards you. In our day-to-day life, we often have to deal with situations that cause us to look at ourselves from a 'we are failures perspective'. This especially happens when we fail to attain a specific goal. Self-love in this case is greatly valuing you despite your weaknesses, failures, and shortcomings. Self-love does not mean that you are oblivious of your mistakes or weaknesses but rather you know that as a human being you will fail and being bold enough to love and appreciate yourself despite this.

Before we start learning how to practice self-love, let us understand how you stand to benefit by practicing self-love.

How You Benefit From Loving Yourself Unconditionally

Practicing self-love has the following benefits:

Helps you accept any outcome: When you practice self-love, you know you are worth and deserve respect; thus, you learn to accept yourself through everything.

When you fully love and accept yourself, you recognize rejection or negative outcome from a given activity as a redirection to take a different route. Instead of beating yourself up over a failure or rejection, you accept the situation, learn from it, and move on with your life. Negative outcomes do not devastatingly affect you because you greatly value yourself and you do not attach the value on any particular outcome.

You learn how to accept yourself: When you love who you are, you accept whom you are. After learning how to practice self-love, you become aware of your strengths and weaknesses, and learn to accept both of them by realizing how unique you are. You stop seeking to be what you are not and instead learn to accept who you are and then start working on becoming the person you want to be.

Helps you deal with negativity from others: As you practice self-love, the opinions of those around you (especially when that opinion is negative) stops bearing immense value. The value you place on their opinions reasonably decreases.

You evaluate the things you spend your time on and discover things that are most important to you. With this, you gain confidence that what you are doing matters, which helps you hold less value to what people consider to matter to you.

Increases your self-confidence: Practicing self-love helps improve our inner voice and power. When you practice self-love, you tune your inner voice to positivity. This helps boost your confidence. You also focus on your positive traits, which boosts your self-confidence and charisma.

Enables you to set clear priorities:

After practicing self-love, you become conscious of how you spend your time and the things you spend it on. With this awareness, your priorities change and you align yourself with what you deem most important. You evaluate everything you are spending your time on and when you realize you are spending your time on things that don't matter much, you change accordingly.

Increases the amount of love we receive from others:

This is because after practicing self-love, you recognize what love is. You learn to focus on the positive aspects of every person and cut people some slack knowing that just like you, they have weaknesses. This increases the feeling of mutual love. It also helps increase your ability to accept love offered by others by accepting you are lovable **and making** you able to recognize love and accept love offered to you.

Makes us happier: After practicing self-love, you accept that you have flaws. With this understanding, you can work on improving your flaws as well as your strengths. For the things you cannot change, you accept that you are not perfect and this realization enables you not to hold on what you cannot do. This is likely to make you a happier person.

You understand yourself better: Self-love helps you understand yourself. It also helps you learn the things that matter to you and enables you to understand why you make mistakes and how each aspect of your life triggers different emotions within you.

By practicing self-love, you learn to appreciate your flaws and work on your strengths to make yourself a better person.

As you have read above, by practicing self-love, you stand to benefit greatly. However, in order to start enjoying these benefits, you first need to learn how to practice self-love. Learning how to practice self-love is a process and to practice self-love, you have to go through various steps. Following is a 21-day guide to practicing self-love.

3. 21 DAY ACTION PLAN FOR LEARNING THE ART OF SELF LOVE

The following are day-to-day steps you have to follow to learn how to practice self-love. At the end of this 21-day self-love action plan, you should be in a position where you can effortlessly practice self-love and derive all the benefits it brings with it:

Day 1-7: Laying the Foundation

In the next seven days, you will be laying the foundation you need to practice immense self-love.

Day 1: Understanding Self-Love

The first step to learning how to love you is having an understanding of what self-love is. Understanding what self-love is will help you know why you need it. Therefore, the first step is defining self-love from a personal perspective.

How to do it

1. The first thing you need to do is determine if you have been practicing self-love. You can do this by listing the normal life situations you go through that can show if you appreciate yourself and if you find yourself worthy. For example, consider the following questions:

Do the negative things people say to you get to you?

Do you beat yourself too hard when you fail to achieve your goals?

Do you do things that matter to you?

Can you tune out negative energy from the outside world?

If you realize you have not been practicing self-love, find a strong 'why' for why you should practice self-love. How will self-love help you? Revisit the benefits of self-love and make a short list of those that ring true to you. This will motivate you to learn how to practice self-love.

2. The second thing you need to do is understand the dangers of not practicing self-love. Learning the dangers of lacking self-love will remind you 'why' self-love is important. Lack of self-love can lead to harmful choices that include the following:

*It can lead to reliance on other people's opinions for validation.

*It can also lead to deprivation of happiness. When you lack self-love, you tend to absorb all the negative energy around you. This ends up blocking your happiness

*Lack of self-love also hinders emotional healing. To be happy, you have to forgive yourself for any wrong doings. A lack of self-love prevents this.

3. The third thing you have to do is understand the existence of negative energy in the outside world. This will help you understand the necessity of self-love. Understand that although you may hear negative comments from other people, this should not set you off.

Realize the need to learn to brush off this negative energy without letting it bruise your feelings. Identify the need to learn how to practice self-love and recognize your readiness to learn how to do it. Prepare yourself psychologically for this process and be ready to learn.

Day 2: Getting To Know Yourself

Getting to know yourself will help you know your strengths. In return, this will help you see why you are worthy and deserving of appreciation. It will boost how you see yourself and the value you attach to yourself.

How to do it

Dedicate five minutes to focusing on yourself: Give yourself the gift of time. Do not feel as if you are wasting this time; enjoy the moment. Take a journal and list your strengths and positive attributes. This process may be hard if for a long time, you have been continuously looking down upon yourself. Just take your time to find something positive in your life. This could include the following:

I am a friendly and sociable person.

I am a good time manager

I can think on my feet

I am innovative

I have a big heart that seeks to help those in difficulties

I am bright and smart

While making this list, ensure you are specific. Do not use general adjectives. For instance, instead of writing "I am caring" you can write the following "Each time I see someone struggling, I take time to know what that person is going through and do my level best to help that person out."

When you finish creating the list, go through your points. However minor they may be, understand that each single one of them is a clear reason why you deserve love and respect.

After listing your points, rise up and go to the mirror. Take your time to look at the image staring back at you. Absorb what you are seeing. Admire the person staring back at you, look yourself in the eyes, and tell yourself that 'you love you.' Self-admiration will boost your confidence.

Go to work and if during the day, anything happens that might pull you back to self-loathing, recite the "I love you" mantra. This will help clear your negative thoughts. At the end of the day, take time to reevaluate yourself. Take note of how you feel. Set a goal to write each positive aspect in your life. This will help you know your progress.

Day 3: Improving Your Inner Voice

Improving your inner voice will help you tune off negativity by creating positive affirmations against the negative thoughts you may have.

How to do it

Love Yourself: 21 day plan for learning "self-love"

1. Stand up and assume a comfortable posture. Focus on your general feeling and how you are feeling; are you relaxed or do you feel energetic? Tune your concentration to breathing and focus on the sequence of your breaths. This will help you become attentive.

2. Understand today's focus as 'improving your inner voice.' Try to understand what your inner voice does to you. This will help you understand why you need to work on improving your inner voice.

Our inner voice affects how we see ourselves and how we see others. Identify the need to improve your inner voice, write down the ways you can do it, and expound on each one of them. This may include the following:

Overcoming negative beliefs about yourself

*Avoiding perfectionism

*Discarding your negative filter

*Focusing on the positive aspects of your

life

Understand the existence of negative energy both from within yourself and from the outside world. This will help you understand why you need to improve your inner voice.

Determine if you hold any negative beliefs about yourself. You can do this by asking yourself these questions.

Do you ever have regrets about something in your past?

Do you hate yourself for lacking a certain thing or trait?

Do you ever feel like you are not good enough? You may hate yourself for a mistake or failure you made in the past.

Identify how these beliefs and thoughts affect you in your daily life. This will help you understand why you need to shower yourself with self-love.

3. Find out if you work towards perfection. This will help you see how perfectionism affects your general life. Find out how you

feel when you are less than perfect. Understand the effort you put in your daily life activities even if you fail to attain your expected perfection. This will help you learn self-appreciation even on minor things. Promise yourself to consider the effort you put into something rather than focusing on the outcome.

4. Discard your negative filter by focusing only on the positive things in your life rather than the negative ones. Try to look at everything in your life from a different perspective: a better perspective. This improves your psychological and emotional state by creating positivity in everything. Even when everything seems to be going wrong, try to find a single positive aspect you can focus on.

5. Rewrite your internal script. When you notice you have negative thoughts about yourself, accept these thoughts first, and then try to determine their source, before moving on to rewriting each negative thought with a positive one. For example, if you forget to buy something you needed, accept that you forgot to buy sugar, but

understand you are a human being prone to mistakes. This will tune your mind into having a positive approach on each matter, which will help get rid of general negativity in your life.

6. At the end of the day, take time to reevaluate yourself. This will help you notice if you are making any progress. Take note of how you feel. Did you notice any other positive aspect in your life? Add it to the previous list – this will grow your list of why you are worthy and deserving of appreciation.

Day 4: Recognizing Love

What does love feel like? Recognizing love will help you know whether you have been practicing self-love and know when you are practicing self-love.

How to do it

Start your day with mindful breathing. Close your eyes and focus your thoughts on the sequence of your breaths. Take a slow deep breath then exhale slowly. This will help heighten your concentration. Take note of your today's point of focus

As stated earlier, understanding what love is or being able to recognize these feelings may be quite difficult if you have been constantly looking down on yourself.

Practicing loving-kindness mindfulness will help you unveil the feelings of love. It will equip you with tools you need to practice self-love. Below is how to practice loving-kindness mindfulness.

1. Assume a comfortable sitting posture.

2. Focus your concentration on your breathing, take a slow deep breath, and then slowly exhale it. This will help you focus on your breathing.

3. As you continue breathing, create positive affirmations that you will repeat in your mind. Identify any negative feelings or thoughts you may incur after reciting each affirmation and identify their **source**.

4. Think of yourself. Identify the feelings that come along with thinking about you.

If any negative thoughts arise, replace them with positive affirmations.

Day 5: Becoming Emotionally Honest

We often fake how we feel in order to be accepted. Emotional dishonesty is one of the threats to practicing self-love and achieving happiness. It is also one of the reasons why you think you are not good enough. You cannot be happy if you are not honest with your emotions. Emotional honesty helps you break the circle of fear and build one of self-appreciation by enabling you to know your true self.

How to do it

1. Start your day with mindful breathing. Close your eyes, take a deep slow breath, and then slowly exhale it. Take note of the changes occurring on and within your body as you breathe. This will help you focus on the current situation. Take note of today's point of focus.

2. Identify times in your life when you have been emotionally dishonest with

yourself; such as the time you lied to yourself about how you feel about liking a person you dislike or feeling sad but acting happy. This will help you realize the negative effects of emotional dishonesty.

3. Identify why you try to numb your feelings and what you do to numb them. Perhaps you try to numb your feelings so you can act strong or feel strong and you may be numbing your feelings by getting drunk, binge shopping, or engaging in other unhealthy behaviors.

4. Try to understand the need for emotional honesty by revisiting its benefits that include fostering courage, creating connection, and eliminating garbage. This will give you the motivation to be honest with yourself. Set an intention to be emotionally honest with yourself today henceforth.

5. During the day, identify various emotions you experience during that day; this could be hatred or sadness. Find out if you have been emotionally honest with yourself. For the negative emotions, find

their source, and then try developing a way to curb them.

For example, you can find out why you hate a person or thing, and then start seeking ways to stop hating it or them. You may choose to focus on a single positive aspect in the beginning. This will help unveil other positive aspects.

At the end of the day, take time to reevaluate yourself to see if you have adhered to the previous steps. This will help you note your progress.

Day 6: Becoming Real

Being real is one of the things we struggle with in our day-to-day lives. Sometimes we hide our true selves to avoid being hurt again. Even so, being real helps build trust in ourselves. To become real, we need to understand its benefits. This will act as the motivation that will encourage you to practice self-love. The benefits of being real include:

Compassion: Being real helps us learn how to be compassionate towards ourselves. Speaking our minds helps us love ourselves and able to achieve the outcome we desire.

Bravery: Being true to yourself teaches you to be courageous and strong. When you are true to yourself, you let others know when you do not approve of something without fear of judgment or rejection.

Comfort: When you openly express yourself, you become comfortable knowing some weight is now off your chest.

Positivity: Learning to trust your inner voice helps you realize the benefit of being real. This motivates you to surround yourself with people who encourage you to be your true self, which ends up building positivity.

How to be real

1. Start by mindful breathing. Take a slow deep breath then exhale slowly. This will help bring your focus to what you are doing. Take note of the topic you will base

your focus on today.

2. Identify the number of times you have been real and spoken out your mind and feelings. Identify how this made you feel. Did it boost your confidence? How did it make you feel? This will help you understand the need to be real. Once you do this, implement the following steps:

*Maintain a journal where you write your feelings; write down the various experiences you experience in life and whether you spoke your mind in each of them. This will act as an encouragement to speak up your mind whenever the chance presents itself.

*Practice mirror work; learn to create a similar image of the feelings inside you by speaking out exactly how you feel

*Set the intention for that day as speaking your mind. If you do not approve of something, make it known. This will boost your confidence and help boost your happiness.

*At the end of the day, reevaluate yourself to see if you have adhered to your previous steps. This will help you know if you are making any progress.

Day 7: Protect Yourself

Protecting yourself means eliminating all the negative energy surrounding you. If you keep the company of people who keep looking down on you or degrading you, it slows your healing process and progress towards practicing self-love. For this reason, you need to do something about all the negative people and stimuli around you.

How to learn to protect yourself

1. Start each process by mindful breathing. Take a slow deep breath and then exhale slowly. Do this for five minutes and take note of the changes occurring in your body as you do this. This will help heighten your concentration on what you are doing. Take note of your today's point of focus.

2. Identify people in your life who create negative energy. For instance, consider

people who say negative things that really hurt you. Identify the emotions these people cause. This will help you realize the need to protect yourself from such characters.

3. Understand the need to get rid of them. There is not enough time in your life to spend time on people who drain you of your happiness. Therefore, detach from anyone you feel is a threat to your happiness.

Day 8-14: Continuity

Here is what you shall be doing for the next 7 days:

Day 8: Identify Your Priorities

Identifying the things that matter to you will help you know what you need to focus on to increase your happiness.

How to identify your priorities

1. Start your day with mindful breathing. Take a slow deep breath then slowly exhale. Take note of the changes occurring in your body, as you do this. For example,

notice the rise and fall of your chest. Once you are mindful, identify your point of focus for the day.

2. Create a list of things that matter to you. Ask yourself this question; what do I value most? Create a list of all things that matter most to you.

3. Understand the need to avoid participating in negativity-laced activities that pull you down. This will help boost your self-confidence. Participating in activities that tamper with your happiness promotes feelings of inadequacy. You should therefore work towards avoiding such activities. Instead, from today onwards, only do things that you enjoy.

At the end of the day, evaluate yourself and determine if you adhered to your principles, and if you did not, do not scold yourself. Accept it and commit to being better next time. Reevaluating yourself will help you see if you are making progress.

Day 9: Forgive Yourself

Forgiveness is a major step towards

learning self-appreciation and self-love. We often scold ourselves and hate ourselves for our past failures and mistakes. We cannot love ourselves if we keep looking down on ourselves. To practice self-love, you thereby need to take a step towards forgiving yourself.

How to forgive yourself

1. Start with mindful breathing. Take a deep slow breath then slowly let it out. Take note of the changes occurring in your body as you do this. This will help heighten your concentration. Once you are calm, you can focus on today's task.

2. Accept you have made several mistakes in your life. This will help you reconcile with yourself. Denying that you have failed will only make the healing process more difficult. 3. Create a list of the various mistakes you have made so far in your life. This could include the following:

*Failing your exams

*Not qualifying for a promotion at work

4. Understand that you are a human being and that you are prone to making mistakes. Learn to take failures as opportunities to learn. If you fail to achieve something, take it as a chance to learn to be better in your next encounter. This will help reduce the hatred you feel towards yourself for your failures.

To better your life, allow yourself to look past your mistakes. You can do this by looking into each of your past failure and concentrating on the effort you exerted as you tried to achieve something better.

For example, for failing in your exams, take note of the effort you put into studying. Appreciate yourself for that. From this day henceforth, set the intention of focusing on your current life and look past your failures.

Day 10: Become Mindful

Mindfulness is a state of awareness whereby you take note of emotions, feelings, and everything around you. Mindfulness is one of the key steps towards practicing self-love and self-appreciation. When you are mindful, you become aware of what you want, feel, or think.

This helps you in a number of ways that include like enabling you take note of degrading thoughts and redirecting them. You also become mindful of who you are and able to use this knowledge to be what you **want to be** rather than what others want for you.

How to become mindful

1. Take a slow deep breath then slowly let it out. Take note of the changes occurring in your body as you do this.

2. Identify the need of mindfulness in your life. Ask yourself this question; how does mindfulness benefit me? Revisit the benefits of mindfulness. This will act as motivation to practice mindfulness.

3. Try identifying the times in your life when you practiced mindfulness. How did this help you? This will help you know why you need to practice mindfulness. Set that day and each day after to be mindful of

everything you are doing.

4. At the end of the day, reevaluate yourself to see if you have adhered to what you had set to. This will help you know if you are progressing towards your end goal: self-love.

Day 11: Discover The Power Of Fun

Having fun will enable you to loosen up. Engage in activities that are fun and ones that boost your mood. When you are happy, you are very unlikely to fall back to looking down on yourself and focusing on your failures or weaknesses. You instead focus on the brighter side of life, which boosts your happiness.

How to have fun

1. Understand the benefits fun brings with it: list the benefits of having fun. This may include the following:

Having fun boosts confidence: confidence is very central to building self-love. Fun helps boost the level of endorphins in the body. Endorphins act as neurotransmitters that send message of confidence and satisfaction to the brain. This in return results in a more cheerful and self-assured you.

*Having fun is also good for de-stressing. When you are having fun, you focus on the positive side of life rather than the negative one. A hobby helps you experience what life has to offer.

2. Identify fun activities you can engage in; this could be swimming or dancing. Once you have this, set out to engage in these activities and while at them, enjoy yourself. This will increase your happiness and positively change how you see yourself.

3. At the end of the day, evaluate yourself and assess how you feel. Determine if you have adhered to the previous steps. You can create a list of all the steps then tick besides each item if you have adhered to them and place a cross next to the ones you have not adhered to. This will help you take note of your progress.

Day 12: Live In Appreciation

Appreciation is being grateful for everything in your life. It involves celebrating your victories no matter how small or big they are, embracing things that make you different by understanding that they are what makes you special, appreciating every single positive aspect in your life ranging from beauty, talents, and brilliance. Practicing appreciation enables you to love your imperfectly perfect self. It reminds you why you are worth.

How to be grateful

1. Try to understand the benefits of appreciation. This will act as motivation for you to practice appreciation. The benefits of appreciation include:

It boosts your self-esteem - It makes you able to focus on the positive aspects, which boosts your self-esteem.

* *Enables you achieve goals faster; appreciation increases determination, energy, and enthusiasm, which all act as driving tools towards achieving your goals.*

2. Make a list of your strengths and victories and then take time to look into each one of them. This will remind you

why you are worthy. For each day, look at this list; it will motivate you to live each day to the **fullest. It is inevitable not to have down days; therefore, learn to find something** positive about each day and focus on this positive.

Day 13: Setting Limits

We live in a busy world where our commitments are immeasurable. Because of this, we often lose track of our limits. It is thereby necessary to set limits about how much we can do in a particular day without wearing ourselves out. This will help you take better care of yourself.

How to set limits

1. Identify things that matter to you. Setting a clear list of your priorities will help you know what you need to do and what you need to say no to. You will love yourself more when you say no to activities or work that deprives you of your happiness, emotional and physical wellbeing.

2. You can do this by doing the following:

Set a strict schedule for waking up and going to sleep.

Make a list of your commitments for the day.

Set a limit on how many hours you need to work in a day.

Day 14: Practice Good Self-Care

When you nourish your body well, you love and appreciate yourself more. Let us look at how to practice good self-care:

How to practice good self-care

*Look at yourself in the mirror and admire your image. You can tell yourself how pretty you look that day or any other positive thing that pops into your mind. This will act as a reminder of why you need to take good care of your body and self.

*Learn to eat a healthy balanced diet. It is also advisable to exercise.

*Practice good hygiene and groom yourself appropriately

As you take care of your mind to get rid of negative thoughts and beliefs, you also need to take good care of your body. The more you practice good self-care, the more you boost your confidence, the more you feel good about yourself and the more you will love yourself.

Day 15-21: Last Leg

Here is what you shall be doing in the last seven days of the 21-day self-love action plan:

Day 15: Avoid Comparisons

Comparing yourself to people is one of the sources of self-loathing. When you do not possess traits other people seem to have, you tend to think that others are better than you while in real sense, being different from the rest of the crowd is what makes us special. Therefore, there is a need to get rid of these comparisons.

How to do this

Create a list of traits you possess that the people around you do not have. This can include the following:

*Generosity

*Patience

*Understanding

Include even the minor traits you have. Look into the benefits of having each of these traits. Concentrating on these traits will remind you of how special you are for being different.

Day 16: Learning Patience

Learning self-love is a process. Self-love is something we need to practice daily but as unfortunate as it sounds, self-love can take long to master, which is why you need to practice patience. Practicing patience boosts self-acceptance and appreciation.

How to practice patience

You can do this by understanding that self-love is a process. This will help you improve the patience you have towards yourself. Therefore, mastering this will take more than a day.

To make the process easier, eliminate the fear and urgency to learn to do it. You can do this by:

Understanding that change is a hard and long process: you cannot change overnight. Accepting this will help you understand why you need to be patient with yourself.

Understanding the importance of pressing on. Remind yourself why you need this by revisiting the <u>benefits of self-love</u>.

Day 17: Live Intentionally

You will love yourself more when you have a strong purpose. When you set a goal you need to achieve, upon achieving it, you appreciate yourself more and love yourself deeper.

How to live intentionally

Set a goal or purpose you need to achieve. This could be living a meaningful and healthy life and then work towards achieving this goal. For example, ensure you eat nutritious meals so you can maintain your health. After a while, evaluate whether you have attained your goal or objective. If you have, you will feel better and love yourself more for attaining such simple goals.

Day 18: Follow Your Passion

Your passion is what you love doing and you would not mind doing it if someone work you up in the middle of the night. Following your passion will boost your self-esteem and boost your moods.

How to follow your passion

Identify things that excite you; this could be drawing or writing, and then set an intention to involve yourself in any of your given activities. Do the things you like but are scared to engage in. In the end, doing these things will boost your confidence and self-esteem, which are key ingredients to practicing self-love.

Day 19: Accept Uncertainty

We live in fear of what the future may hold and constantly allow pain from our past to predict our future and torment our present life. To learn self-love, you need to understand and accept that uncertainty is part of everyday life.

How to accept uncertainty

Let go of your past traumas. To do this, create a list of previous experiences that rob you of your inner peace and torment you. Look into each of them, accept that they happened, and you can do nothing to change them.

Instead of letting them torment you, use them as a learning platform for your betterment. Understand that there exists uncertainty on what the future may hold, but always hope for the best and live in the moment. This will help you attain a state of peace.

Day 20: Let Go Of What You Cannot Change

Some situations in our lives are beyond our ability to alter. To be at peace with yourself, learn to let go of such things otherwise, they will deprive you of the joy of living in the moment.

How to Do this

To let go, you need to look at different situations in your life. Accept the way everything in your life is. For instance, accept your current economic situation; this, however, should not be an excuse to be lazy but rather to be realistic with the situation and the options available to you to make the necessary changes Stop fighting with yourself or wishing things were different; accept where you are and work with what you have to become better.

Day 21: Follow Your Inner Voice

To practice self-love, you need to follow your conscience. When you follow your conscience in undertaking various activities in your life, you gain satisfaction from the results.

How to do this

When you are confused about which choices to make or the path to follow in your life, take a moment, take a deep breath and listen to your conscience. There is always that inner voice guiding us on what to do. Follow it when making choices. Following your deeper small inner voice boosts your confidence and self-esteem. It also helps us accept all the outcomes whatsoever.

Conclusion

Thank you again for purchasing this book!

As you implement this 21-day self-love action plan, also try something new as often as you can out of your normal schedule. For example, if you create specified meals each day of the week, choose to step out of your comfort zone and try a new recipe or add some more spices. See how this works for you. You will feel more satisfied with yourself for making this new discovery: self-satisfaction leads to self-love.

Hey! Do you mind giving your feedback on Amazon by rating and reviewing my book.

I would really appreciate that.

My Other Books

1. Intermittent Fasting: 7 effective techniques of Intermittent Fasting

2. Blockchain Technology : Introduction to Blockchain Technology and its impact on Business Ecosystem

3. DevOps Handbook: Introduction to DevOps and its impact on Business Ecosystem

4. Blockchain Technology & DevOps: Introduction and impact on Business Ecosystem

** If you prefer audible versions of these books, I have few free coupons, drop me a mail at: **valueadd2life@gmail.com.** If available, I would mail you the same.

www.ingramcontent.com/pod-product-compliance
Lightning Source LLC
LaVergne TN
LVHW011859060526
838200LV00054B/4434